DATE DUE			
AP 1'92			
JAN 27 '06			
C 11			

THE SEMINOLES

MARTIN LEE
THE SEMINOLES

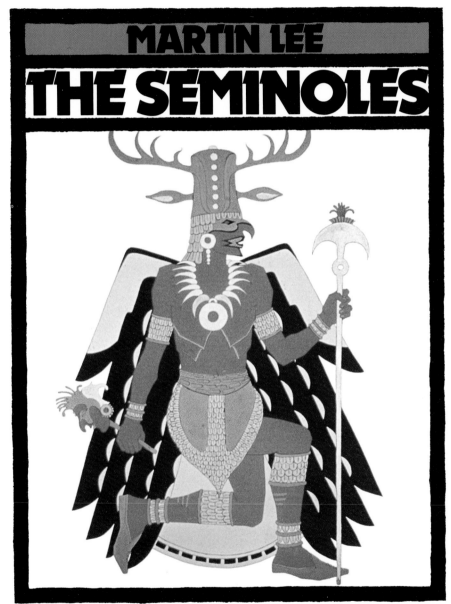

Franklin Watts   New York   London   Toronto   Sydney   A First Book   1989

Library of Congress Cataloging-in-Publication Data

Lee, Martin.
The Seminoles / by Martin Lee.
p. cm.—(First book)
Includes index.
Summary: After a brief tribal history, describes Seminole Indian
life in villages in the Everglades in the past and changes that have
come in modern times.
ISBN 0-531-10752-3
1. Seminole Indians—Social life and customs—Juvenile literature.
2. Indians of North America—Florida—Social life and customs—
Juvenile literature. [1. Seminole Indians. 2. Indians of North
America—Florida.] I. Title. II. Series.
E99.S28L44 1989
975.9'004973—dc20   89-8900   CIP   AC

for Marcia

CONTENTS

Also by Martin Lee

PAUL REVERE

This book tells the story of a proud people.
It is a story of change and survival.

Throughout their history, the Seminoles
had to start over, again and again,
and learn to adapt to new lands. Yet
they developed a way of life that has
lasted to this day.

Modern-day Seminoles live and work in
Oklahoma and on reservations in Florida.
Some still practice the old ways to preserve
their unique culture.

THE BEGINNING

The first people to settle in the Americas were wandering bands of hunters, probably from Asia. Some scientists say they came about fifteen thousand years ago. Others say these early settlers began arriving as early as forty thousand years ago.

They probably crossed the Bering Strait to get here. They came from what is now called Siberia, in the Soviet Union. To the first settlers, the Bering Strait was not a body of water at all, but a wide, dry, windswept plain. Many animals crossed this land in search of food. The hunters depended on these animals for their own food. So the hunters followed them to North America. As the ice cap that covered much of North America spread, the animal herds moved south into the warmer lands of the Americas.

The hunters came too, right into the heart of this unknown continent. They wandered from place to place searching for the herds. Some people moved toward the forests of the east. One of these groups of people was the Muskogee. They settled in what are now the states of Georgia, Alabama, and northern Florida.

The Muskogee settled near the Chattahoochee, Coosa, Flint, and Tallapoosa rivers. Searching for food was easy; so was farming. The Muskogee cleared land for farming by chopping down trees and burning brush. They grew an ample supply of corn, squash, and pumpkins. The women raised the children, and cooked, and made baskets, pottery, and clothing. The men hunted and fished, built buildings, governed, and made war.

The Muskogee population grew steadily and spread over a wide area. The many different Muskogee towns formed a league called a confederacy. The town chiefs, called *mikkos,* met in councils to make laws for all the towns in the confederacy. Soon white men—Europeans—began to arrive and settle in North America. They called the Muskogee *Creeks,* because Muskogee towns were built along rivers and creeks.

Europeans saw America as a source of land and gold. By the mid-1500s, England, Spain, and France were in a race to claim the land of the New World. Unfor-

A MIKKO, MEANING CHIEF OVER CHIEF

A LARGE INDIAN TRADE CANOE
TRAVELING PAST WOODED BANKS ON
THE LOWER MISSISSIPPI RIVER.
THE ARROW INDICATES THE DIRECTION
OF THE CURRENT'S FLOW.

tunately, the Creeks found themselves right in the middle of the struggle.

The Creeks traded with the English colony in Charleston and with the Spanish in Florida. They also traded with the French at New Orleans and Mobile. After a while, the English convinced the Creek Confederacy to join forces against Spain and France and take part in raids of Spanish missions in Florida.

By 1708, English colonists began taking over Creek lands. Because of this, many Creeks who came on the raids in Florida stayed there. Spain granted citizenship and freedom to all Indians who came to Florida. After a while, all the Florida Creeks who separated from the creek Confederacy in the north were called Seminoles. *Seminole* is a word with many meanings. To some, like the English colonists in the 1700s, it meant "runaway." To others, it meant "free" or "wild," like a bear is wild.

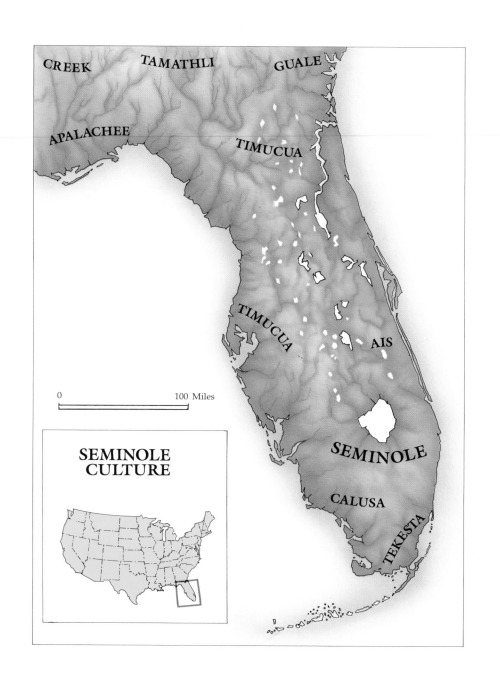

CREEK   TAMATHLI   GUALE

APALACHEE   TIMUCUA

TIMUCUA   AIS

SEMINOLE
CULTURE

SEMINOLE

CALUSA

TEKESTA

0   100 Miles

A NEW HOME FOR A NEW TRIBE

In time, entire Creek villages migrated to the grassy, rolling plains of northern and central Florida to join the Seminoles. The first Seminole settlements in Florida were located along rivers, as were the Creek villages further north.

One of the first important Seminole villages was Cuscowilla. Larger than most villages, Cuscowilla had about thirty family dwellings. Each dwelling consisted of two buildings that stood perhaps 20 yards (18 m) apart.

One of the buildings was divided into two rooms—one for cooking, the other for sleeping. The second building was as long and as wide as the first, but it was higher. It had two floors that were used mostly for storing potatoes, grains, and other foods. The second floor

THIS SEMINOLE VILLAGE SHOWS SOME OF THE
DIFFERENT HOUSE STYLES OF THE INDIANS.
IN THE WARM CLIMATES, SOME OF THE BUILDINGS
WERE OFTEN WITHOUT WALLS; OTHERS WERE BUILT
ON STILTS ABOVE THE MARSHY GROUND.

also had an open, shaded platform at one end that could
be reached by an outside ladder. This platform was re-
served for the head of the family. Here, he received visitors and rested in comfort during the hot summer days.

Each family in Cuscowilla had a small garden by its
house. There was also a common planting area about

2 miles (3.2 km) from town. The whole village farmed this fenced area. Families tended their own clearly marked parts and gathered their own crops for storage. Near the center of the planting area was a common storage building. Each family contributed grain and potatoes to that public food supply. Visitors, like runaway slaves, and tribe members who couldn't care for themselves were welcome to this food.

SEMINOLES TAKING FRUIT TO
THEIR STOREHOUSES

WAR

The Seminoles adjusted well to life in Florida. Their harvests were good, and there was plenty of food. They felt safe.

But the Seminoles, like the Creeks, Chickasaw, Choctaw, and Cherokee to the north, were in the wrong place at the wrong time. They found themselves in the path of an unstoppable force. That force was the growing United States. It wanted the land on which the Seminoles and other Indians lived.

Trouble came to the Creeks first in the form of General Andrew Jackson. Jackson thought the Indian cultures were inferior to his own. He had no respect for Indian rights. In the early 1800s, with the support of the

American government, Jackson attacked Creek villages in Georgia. Among the Creeks who fled to Florida to join the Seminoles there were a mother and her young son, named Osceola.

Meanwhile, land-hungry American settlers were pouring into Florida. Florida still belonged to Spain at this time, but the Spanish government agreed to permit new settlements there on land the Seminoles believed was theirs. Not liking this, the Seminoles raided some of these settlements.

These raids angered the American government. In 1818 Army General Jackson led troops into Florida that attacked and burned Seminole villages. These attacks came to be known as the First Seminole War. Spain did not approve of this armed invasion, but was too weak to stop it. Instead, Spain sold Florida to the United States.

The First Seminole War ended in 1819. A treaty ending the war was signed in 1823. At this time, some Seminoles were forced to resettle in central Florida north of Big Cypress Swamp. The American government promised to protect the Seminole rights to this new land. Still, hundreds of white settlers continued to move onto Seminole lands. The settlers attacked Seminole villages and destroyed the crops.

In 1828, now president, Andrew Jackson signed the Indian Removal Act. This law said that all Indians in the Southeast were to be moved westward, across the Mississippi, to land set aside for them there. The Seminoles refused to leave.

Federal agents came to Florida to persuade the Seminoles to leave. Young Osceola was among those who represented the Seminoles in meetings with the American government. When it was his turn to sign the removal plan, Osceola boldly plunged his knife through the paper. "This is the way I sign," he said. Osceola, then only thirty-two years old, became an important Seminole leader.

A few months after Osceola stabbed the paper, he attacked the American army at Fort King. That same day, American soldiers marching to Fort King were attacked by another Seminole war party. These two actions started the Second Seminole War.

The U.S. government sent troops into the Florida swamps to crush the Seminoles. But the Seminoles struck back. They ambushed and killed small groups of soldiers and took their weapons.

After a few years of fighting, the Americans decided to stop chasing the few hundred remaining Seminoles and the war ended. The war had cost the U.S. government over $20 million and the lives of over fifteen hundred soldiers. The cost was great to the Seminoles as well. Thousands of them were shipped to New

OSCEOLA LEARNED TO HATE THE WHITE
PEOPLE WHEN HIS WIFE, MORNING DEW, WAS
KIDNAPPED BY RAIDING WHITE SETTLERS.

Orleans, then up the Mississippi and Arkansas rivers to Fort Gibson, Oklahoma. Those who remained in Florida fled still deeper into the Everglades wilderness. There they tried to go on with their lives, far from the reaches of American expansion.

LIFE ON THE HAMMOCKS

The Everglades is a flat, low swampland that is covered with slowly flowing water. Here and there are islands called *hammocks,* patches of thick forest. The Seminoles established their new villages on these hammocks.

A typical village had a cluster of eight or ten houses called *chickees,* built around the edge of the land. A chickee is a simple house without walls. It was raised on a platform about 3 feet (1 m) above the ground. The slanting roof was thatched with palmetto leaves, called fronds. The edges of the roof hung over the living area and kept it dry.

Cooking and eating were considered to be group activities. An area in the middle of the village was cleared for the cookhouse and the eating house. In the center

[25]

THE SEMINOLES LIVED ON ISLANDS IN
THE EVERGLADES CALLED HAMMOCKS.
HAMMOCKS ARE SMALL BECAUSE MOST OF
THE EVERGLADES IS SWAMPLAND.

A TYPICAL SEMINOLE HOUSE

of the cookhouse was a large fire pit. Women cooked for the entire village over a fire that was almost always burning.

The eating house was the largest building in the village. Everyone came there to share meals. Regular meals were served to villagers each morning and evening. However, food was always available so people could eat at any time of the day. The eating house also served as a guest house for strangers who came to the village.

The Seminoles found the rich hammock land perfect for farming. Each year after the planting, the Seminole children stationed themselves in the fields to scare away the blackbirds, crows, and jackdaws. At night, the young men and older boys guarded the crops from curious deer, raccoons, and woodchucks.

TWO PEOPLE—HUMAN SCARECROWS—
STAND ON PLATFORMS OVERLOOKING
A CORNFIELD. THEY ARE TRYING TO
KEEP BIRDS AWAY FROM THEIR CROPS.

The Seminoles planted sweet potatoes, pumpkins, melons, and rice, but their main crop was corn. From it, they made many kinds of foods, including different soups. They shucked the corn and mashed and soaked it to make *hominy*. From hominy, the Seminoles made cakes and bread.

Hominy was also the source of a thin corn soup called *sofki*, the most important food in the Seminole diet. At a Seminole meal, everyone ate sofki from one large bowl, using only one spoon. The spoon started with the men, then passed to the boys, and then went to the women and girls.

Many Seminole meals included foods made from a flour called *coontie*. Coontie was made from the long, thick, underground stems of the fernlike arrowroot plant. Seminole children helped their mothers in the preparation of this flour. A favorite coontie preparation was a honey-sweetened, jellylike dessert, something like tapioca pudding.

Game, fowl, and fish were also part of the Seminoles' diet. They ate a variety of meats too. They often feasted on turkey, duck, quail, and venison (deer meat). They sometimes enjoyed opossum, rabbit, and squirrel. Occasionally, bear or gopher was the main course in the eating house.

The Seminoles were skilled hunters. They caught birds, squirrels, and most other small animals in traps or with darts shot through blowguns. Blowguns were made of cane stalks. The darts were slivers of cane or pieces of hardwood.

For larger game and fish, the Seminoles used bows and arrows. The bow was firmly made from a single piece of black locust, hickory, or other springy wood. It took a powerful person to bend one of these bows.

INDIANS CURING FISH AND
GAME ON A BARBEQUE

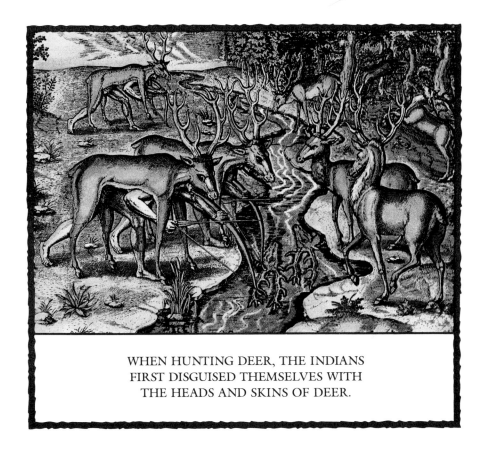

WHEN HUNTING DEER, THE INDIANS
FIRST DISGUISED THEMSELVES WITH
THE HEADS AND SKINS OF DEER.

The bowstring was made from twisted deer hide. Hunters fastened turkey feathers to their arrows with glue made from deer antlers. The arrowheads were made from fish bones. Over the years, as the Seminoles traded with the white settlers, they were able to get brass and sheet iron in the form of kettles, pots, and pans. From them they fashioned tips for their arrows. The hunters

THE SEMINOLES USED BOWS AND ARROWS AND
WERE SKILLED HUNTERS. AFTER THEY BEGAN
TRADING WITH WHITE MEN, THEY SWAPPED THEIR
BOWS AND ARROWS FOR GUNS.

were also able to get guns. They eventually began to prefer the guns to their bows and arrows. After a while, many Seminole hunters had muzzle-loading rifles.

In addition to hunting, fishing, and farming, the Seminoles lived by trading with other tribes and with their white neighbors, particularly the Spanish.

TRADING WITH WHITES GAVE THE SEMINOLES
CLOTH AND BEADS TO MAKE SUCH ITEMS
AS THIS BAG, AND GAVE THEM SILVER TO
MAKE THE BAND ON THIS TURBAN.

At the trading posts, the Seminoles traded alligator hides and deerskins, furs, dried fish, beeswax, and honey. In exchange, they returned to their villages with goods such as coffee, liquors, tobacco, cloth, metal pots, and knives. The Spanish traders treated the Seminoles very well. The Seminoles were entertained by the traders and were served the traders' finest foods and beverages.

For each new generation of Seminoles, the structure of village life was set. Responsibility for most jobs was determined by custom and passed on from parents to children over the years. Men and women had clearly defined tasks. Boys and girls were expected to learn these tasks by watching and helping.

Seminole children were raised to share in the village work as soon as they were ready. Seminole girls were taught by their mothers. They learned all the skills they would need when they became women. Boys were taken in hand by a respected member of the clan, often an uncle or a village elder. He taught them the skills they would need for adulthood. The elder lectured the boys during ceremonies and tribal gatherings.

Seminole children slept on animal skins in the hope that they would take on the qualities of that animal. For example, infant boys might sleep on panther skins because panthers were such skilled hunters. Girls often slept on deerskins to become as gentle and modest as deer.

SEMINOLE CHILDREN HAD MANY RESPONSIBILITIES AND
WERE EXPECTED TO SHARE IN THE WORK OF THE VILLAGE.

There was always much to do in the Seminole village. Apart from the shared tasks of farming and building, men and women had different responsibilities.

It was men's work to hunt, fish, rule the village, make tools and weapons, lead ceremonies, and entertain visitors. Men also made war. War was very important to the Seminoles. When the men were preparing for war, they painted their heads, necks, and breasts with red paint. In battle, they were fierce warriors who defended their territory with great courage. The Seminoles were proud of their bravery. Although they were harsh in combat, the Seminoles were fair to their enemies. They spared their enemies' lives when they could. Like many other Indian tribes, Seminoles enslaved the captured enemy. These prisoners of war could marry Seminole tribe members, and their children would become members of the tribe.

The women had equally important responsibilities in the village. They cooked, cared for the home, raised the children, and made the clothing for everyone in the village. Seminole women made clothing that was both useful and attractive. Seminole housing and diet changed as the people moved south to the warmer climate of the Everglades, and their way of dress changed as well.

One thing a visitor would notice immediately about the Seminole clothing was how bright it was with its

INDIANS PANNING FOR GOLD IN A STREAM

strong colors and bold patterns. The women may have been inspired by the many-colored banded tree snails that lived in the Everglades. Or perhaps the fancy Spanish costumes caught their eye.

Seminole men typically wore long, knee-length shirts over their loincloths. A loincloth is a piece of cloth that passes between the legs and is tied with a wide belt. Their embroidered cotton shirts were buttoned high and were tight around the wrists.

On special occasions, the Seminole men wore handwoven sashes. These were worn over one shoulder, hanging down to the waist. The sashes were made from yarn that was unraveled from coarse cloth. The sashes had glass beads woven into Vs, Ws, or diamond-shaped designs.

The men wore one or more bright yellow or red scarves around their necks. Because their shirts had no pockets, the men sometimes kept money knotted in the corner of a scarf. They wore silver bracelets fastened by cords, and leather belts around their waists. The belts held pouches for hunting gear.

In the Everglades, the men usually went barefooted. But in northern Florida, where the weather was often cooler, they wore moccasins and deerskin leggings. The leggings protected them from the brambles and underbrush.

A TYPICAL SEMINOLE OUTFIT

SEMINOLE CLOTHING WAS
BRIGHTLY COLORED AND FESTIVE.

Seminole men often wore turbans made from pieces of wool blanket or from smaller shawls. Turbans were often decorated with stones, beads, silver ornaments, porcupine quills, or bird wings. Seminole warriors commonly placed eagle, hawk, or owl feathers in the turban.

Seminole men often wore earrings made of silver, brass, or glass beads. Some pierced several holes in each ear. Some men pierced their noses and wore silver ornaments there.

Seminole women dressed in an equally festive manner. Women's shirts, which were usually white, were waist-length and had no buttons. Often, the collars and cuffs were embroidered in yellow, red, and brown. Women wore knee or calf-length skirts made from strips of brightly colored calico and gingham. The strips were pieced together to form many different shapes and patterns. Women usually went barefooted.

Necklaces were very important to Seminole women. They proudly wore as many of them as they could. To the women, wearing many necklaces showed their wealth or popularity. Necklaces were made from string upon string of brightly colored beads the women had collected since they were girls. The women wore enormous numbers of necklaces, sometimes 10 to 15 pounds (4½ to 7 kg) at a time! Women could often be seen wearing as many as two hundred strings of large beads gathered around their necks and hanging down their backs. Under the beads, the Seminole women wore silver necklaces that were made from European and American coins pounded until they were thin.

Seminole women wore nothing on their heads, but they wore their hair in a unique style. The women's hair was gathered in a shape that stuck out from the head. It looked as if they were wearing wide-brimmed hats. The women wore bangs in the front. Little girls wore their hair braided and tied with a ribbon.

Women wore rings and sometimes earrings. The rings were large and made of silver. Women had their ears pierced and wore slivers of palmetto wood for earrings.

Children dressed differently from their parents. The youngest wore no clothes at all. Young boys wore only long shirts. Young girls wore simple dresses. On special occasions, the girls fastened decorative collars to their dresses.

In addition to making the clothing, raising the children, and preparing the food, Seminole women in northern Florida made pottery. On the hammocks in the Everglades, women wove mats and baskets from cane and palmetto stalks. The baskets were used in the preparation of foods. Pounded corn was sifted through the flat baskets the women made.

WOMEN PROUDLY WORE AS MANY NECKLACES AS THEY COULD. THIS SEMINOLE WOMAN IS PUTTING ON THE TWENTY-SECOND DOUBLE STRAND OF BEADS.

SOME OF THE BALL GAMES PLAYED BY
THE SOUTHEASTERN INDIANS

The Seminoles did not work all the time. The men and women often played games. One game that was popular for a while was called *chunkey*. The women and men played it together. The object of the game was to strike the top of a 25 to 30 foot (7.5 to 9 m) pole with a ball. If a ball struck the cow's skull or carved fish placed on the very top of the pole, four points were scored. A strike within 5 or 10 feet (1.5 m to 3 m) of the top was worth two points. The men used sticks with nets on one end, and the women used their hands.

THE SEMINOLE WAY

The Seminoles, like all people, looked for ways to explain the world around them. They believed that animals and plants had magic powers. The Seminoles believed the earth was flat and that the sky rose and fell above it. The moon was home to a man and a dog. The Seminoles believed in a world full of invisible spirits—some good, some not so good.

The *Preserver of Breath,* who gave life and took it away, was the greatest spirit. The *Fire Spirit* was his messenger. *Corn Mother* was the goddess of farming. *Thunder* was the rain and war god. Lesser spirits lived in the trees and in streams and ponds. Spirits living in the water could bring on or withhold rain. The evil *water panthers* and *horned rattlesnakes* were powerful water monsters that would wrap around swimmers and drown them in the stream. *Little people* who lived in the forests would sometimes help lost boys find their way home safely. Other times, they could be tricksters.

Ceremonies played a large part in Seminole life. Water and fire were very sacred. Most ceremonies had to do with one or the other. For example, newborn children were immediately bathed in the cold, running water of a stream. This would be the first of many cold baths they would take in their lives for ceremonial purposes.

CEREMONIES WERE IMPORTANT IN SEMINOLE LIFE. HERE THE INDIANS ARE CONSECRATING THE SKIN OF A STAG TO THE SUN.

Also, as mentioned earlier, a fire was always burning in the village. The fire was only put out for a short time during the most important celebration of the year—the Green Corn Ceremony.

The Green Corn Ceremony, or *Busk,* began when the corn reached the roasting ear stage in late June or mid-July. It lasted for about a week. It was a celebration of new beginnings. It was a time for settling arguments and repaying debts. It was also a time for cleaning houses and throwing away old things.

During the Green Corn Ceremony, the men ate nothing but drank teas. They believed that the drinking would make them pure and powerful. Those who gulped down the tea, a quart (1 liter) at a time, became sick to their stomachs. Soon after drinking, the men vomited. They believed that this cleansed their bodies and gave them the energy to perform the Corn Dances all night long.

There were over forty different Corn Dances. Each was accompanied by music and singing. Women joined the men for these dances. During the dances, women wore tortoise shell rattles to keep a steady beat. The men did the singing.

The festivities included other events and games. One game the Seminoles played during the Green Corn Ceremony was stickball. We play stickball today. But the game the Seminoles played was much different from ours.

MANY INDIAN TRIBES, IN ADDITION TO THE SEMINOLES,
HAD GREEN CORN CEREMONIES. IN THIS PARTICULAR
TRIBE'S RITUAL, CHANTING SHAMANS STOMP AND WARRIORS
CIRCLE A COOKING FIRE WHILE CARRYING CORNSTALKS.

Seminole stickball was really more like the modern game of lacrosse, only much fiercer. It was a team game played on a very large field—even larger than our modern football field. Stickball was a rough game, with blocking and tackling.

Stickball was not only played during the Green Corn Ceremony. Seminole villages played against each other in a kind of mock war. It was a way to strengthen themselves for real war. Also, in a more gentle form of the game, men played against women. Couples played this less violent stickball as part of their courtship.

The long Green Corn Ceremony made everyone pure from tea-drinking, dancing, and playing. On the last day, all fires in the village were put out. Then someone laid out wood for a new fire. Next, four perfect ears of green corn were placed on top of the wood. The Seminoles said prayers and magic words, and the new sacred fire was lit to burn the corn. From this fire, all other fires in the village were rekindled.

Then the men ate fresh, green corn that had been gathered and prepared by the women. This was an exciting time, because the men hadn't eaten any fresh corn since the last harvest. When the four perfect ears of corn had been completely burned and the men had taken four rounds of medicine, the Green Corn Ceremony came to an end. With the end of the festivities came the end of the year. A new Seminole year began.

SEMINOLE YOUTHS EXERCISING

TO MODERN TIMES

The Seminoles who left Florida to go to Oklahoma faced hardships right from the start. The American government arranged to have them live with the Creeks, who were already settled there. But neither nation was happy with this plan. By now, the two tribes had become very different from each other. The Seminoles wanted their own nation with their own laws.

Some of the Seminoles went to live temporarily with the Cherokee Nation. Others remained at Fort Gibson. But the living conditions there were terrible. Crowded into barracks, the Seminoles suffered from sickness and starvation. Many died.

In 1845, some land in Oklahoma was set aside for the Seminoles alone. Although many Seminoles now

THE SEMINOLES WHO LEFT
FLORIDA TO HEAD WEST HAD
A DIFFICULT TIME. CONDITIONS
WERE HARSH AND MANY PEOPLE
DIED ALONG THE WAY.

settled on this land, others spread throughout the new western territories.

The Seminole Nation, consisting of more than twenty towns, was officially established in 1856. Wewoka, Oklahoma, was its capital.

Today, the Seminoles in Oklahoma live in fourteen towns and are citizens of the United States. They have a tribal government that meets at Wewoka. The principal chief and a council advise the U.S. government on matters concerning the well-being of the Oklahoma Seminole Nation.

The Oklahoma Seminoles today live in modern houses in modern communities. They live as neighbors among all other citizens of the state. But many still speak Muskogee, hold on to many of their beliefs, and follow their traditional religion.

The few hundred Seminoles who remained in Florida were not left alone to live in peace. White settlers kept invading their villages looking for runaway slaves. Federal agents kept trying to convince the Indians to join the others in Oklahoma. Not many Seminoles, however, were interested.

In 1855, a group of federal land surveyors trampled corn fields and ruined fruit trees at a Seminole settlement. Chief Billy Bowlegs held a meeting of tribal leaders. They decided to strike back. A Seminole war party attacked the camp. This was the start of what some called the Third Seminole War.

The fighting lasted three years. In 1858, the U.S. government offered to pay the Seminoles to leave Florida. Only Billy Bowlegs and 123 followers took the offer. A few hundred others refused to go. They remained in the Everglades. These Seminoles were the ancestors of the modern Seminoles who live in Florida today.

THE THIRD SEMINOLE WAR WAS THE RESULT OF WHITES RUINING THE FIELDS AND TREES OF A SEMINOLE SETTLEMENT IN FLORIDA. THE INDIANS STRUCK BACK AT THIS LACK OF REGARD FOR THEIR LAND.

CHIEF BILLY BOWLEGS WAS INVOLVED
IN THE THIRD SEMINOLE WAR.

THE SEMINOLE WAY OF LIFE TODAY IS A COMBINATION OF THE OLD WAYS AND THE NEW. THIS CLASSROOM IN A SEMINOLE SCHOOL IS A PERFECT EXAMPLE OF THIS BLEND. NOTICE THE TRADITIONAL SEMINOLE HOUSE IN THE BACKGROUND WITH THE MORE MODERN PLAY EQUIPMENT.

Today many of Florida's Seminoles live on three federal Indian reservations. Big Cypress Reservation is in the middle of the Everglades. Brighton Reservation is located on the west side of Lake Okeechobee. Hollywood Reservation is near Fort Lauderdale. About two thousand Seminoles live on these reservations. There is a tribal council, much like the one in Oklahoma. The council members meet with U.S. government representatives to deal with Florida Seminole tribal affairs.

MANY SEMINOLES TODAY CHOOSE
TO LIVE THE TRADITIONAL WAY IN
CHICKEES IN SMALL VILLAGES.

Many Seminoles who live on the Florida reservations raise cattle and work on truck farms and in lumber camps. Others are construction workers and mechanics. Still others work in the tourist business selling handicrafts.

Although many Florida Seminoles have modern ways of life, others still proudly maintain the old traditions. These people practice their ancient religious beliefs and try to live according to the old ways. They choose to live in chickees in small villages encircled by tall wooden fences.

Some of the men and women dress as Seminoles used to, in long, colorful shirts and patchwork dresses. The women even style their hair as their ancestors once did, and they still wear many strings of beads. These Seminoles are working to keep old arts and crafts alive for future generations.

If you were to visit a traditional Seminole village today in early summer, you might hear the rattles and the singing. You might see men and women dancing the old dances late into the night. You would be a modern witness to a very old celebration. You would see the Green Corn Ceremony.

FOR FURTHER READING

Bierhorst, John. *Doctor Coyote: A Native American's Aesop's Fables*. New York: Macmillan, 1987.

Freedman, Russell. *Indian Chiefs*. New York: Holiday House, 1987.

George, Jean Craighead. *The Talking Earth*. New York: Harper & Row, 1983.

Mayo, Gretchen Will. *Star Tales: North American Indian Stories about the Stars*. New York: Walker, 1988.

Wallin, Luke. *In the Shadows of the Wind*. New York: Bradbury Press, 1984.

Wheeler, M. J. *First Came the Indians*. New York: Macmillan, 1983.

INDEX